The Future of the Colored Race in America

by William Aikman

I0420256

THE FUTURE OF THE COLORED RACE IN AMERICA.

BY WILLIAM AIKMAN, Pastor of the Hanover Street Presbyterian Church, Wilmington, Delaware.

In whatever way the present civil war in America shall result, it is certain that the future condition of the colored race in this country will be the question over-mastering all others for many years to come. It has already pushed itself into the foremost place. However it may be true, that slavery and the negro were not the proximate causes of this war, no one who gives any candid thought to the matter can fail to recognize the fact, that back of all, this stands as the grand first occasion of it. Had there been no slavery, there would have been no war. General Jackson was only partly right when he said, that while in his day the tariff was made the pretext of secession, and that by and by slavery would take its place, but that neither would be the true motive of disunion; that a desire for a separate confederacy was the final cause. This was evidently correct, yet had slavery not stood in this country there would not have come into being that peculiar state of society which now lives in the Southern States, and which demands for its very existence that it should rule alone. Slavery has created an aristocracy, not of numbers, but of wealth and power, which bears with all the social forces. While the slave-holder are but a very small minority of the whole people, yet by the force of their wealth and the fact of their being slave owners, they hold all the political power, and indeed, sweep out of existence any opposition. There are, with very rare exceptions throughout the whole South, but two classes--free and slave, or we may say, slave-holders and slaves, for the non slave-holders are completely lost and absorbed in the all-controlling element which is above them; they work in with it, and are indeed a part of it. As slavery called this aristocracy into being, and created its power, so it holds it in being; anything which strikes at slavery strikes at the root of this power; to destroy slavery would be to blot it out of existence.

Around this point the whole contest is waged, and from it alone every movement is to be interpreted. In the days of South Carolina nulification the tariff was indeed the pretext of rebellion, and the true motive was a separate government and the perpetuation of the power of the dominant class, but this power depended wholly upon the status of slavery, and so, back of all slavery was even then the thought, and to strengthen slavery the great end. In this we find the accurate explanation of the studied and persistent efforts to extend and perpetuate it, not because it is admired in itself, or because it is seen to be politically or socially beneficial, but because it is the cornerstone of a valued social state. A friend, some years ago sailing down the Potomac, was engaged in conversation with the captain of the boat, a blunt, bluff Southerner, and looking over the beautiful scenery on either side of the river, said, "Why do you Virginians hold on to slavery? it is a thousand pities that such a country as this should be so poorly used." "I know it," replied the captain, "slavery does ruin the state; but the fact is, we like it; a man feels good when he owns twenty or fifty negroes, and can say to one go, and he goes, and to another come and he comes." Here the whole philosophy of the social state of the South is in a nut-shell. To abandon slavery is to abandon a position which has been held as a tenure of nobility for two hundred years. Nothing but the direst necessity will bring it about. It will never be given voluntarily up; the whole force of human nature is against it relinquishment. As well might the nobility of England be expected to throw up their titles and their coronets on persuasion. Here is a case where argument has no power. You may exhaust it, you may prove slavery to be wrong morally, wrong socially, wrong politically, you may prove it to a demonstration that it is an economic blunder of the most gigantic proportions, you may make it clear as sunlight that it is demoralizing and ruinous, but you have done absolutely nothing toward its abolishment. Here and there a truly conscientious man or woman, under the great pressure of duty, will consent to the liberation of their slaves; but the public conscience is so ethereal a thing that it can be touched by no appeals of duty or obligation, and will never force a community up to any great work, least of all to such a work as this.

The effect of emancipating one's slaves upon the social position of the master, has been seen over and over again; the hour when the bonds are broken and freedom is given is the hour when all the former associations are given up; expatriation and banishment are the inevitable results. The generous, or the conscientious emancipator at once becomes an exile; he has sunk at once out of an aristocracy whose titular power he gave up the moment he ceased to be a slave-holder, and he cannot comfortably abide in even his old home. Here is the explanation of the vast and unexpected power put forth by this rebellion, of the unconquered will, of the enormous sacrifices endured; here is the explanation of the seeming insanity of the struggle, of the unwarrantableness of its acts, of the demoniac fierceness of its rage, and the diabolical malignity and cruelty of its method of war; it is the death struggle of a great social element, for which to be conquered is to be ruined and swept out of existence.

No man understood this so well or so soon as the great Nullifier. He was a thinker and a philosopher, and so with great logical consistency he became the early author of the doctrine of slavery as now almost universally held at the South. He startled and shocked the men of his time by his bold positions in respect to that institution, and was far in advance of his time in his assertions of its inherent rightfulness, and the determination not only to terminate, but to extend, strengthen and perpetuate it. He was a nullifier because a slave-holder in principle. The one grew out of, and was a part of the other. The maintenance of an oligarchy was the ultimate end, that rested on slavery, and so "state rights" so called, and the divine right of slavery went hand in hand.

This is strikingly evident in the history of the present war. The rapid rise, and the culmination of rebellion in act, was preceded by the new annunciation of these doctrines of Calhoun on slavery. We remember well how strange it sounded, and how startling in the General Assembly of only 1856, when slavery was declared an institution not needing to be defended or apologized for, but to be praised and justified as truly an ordinance of God as marriage, or the filial relation. The church had known no such doctrine before, and then spued it out of her mouth, but it was gravely held and fiercely and impudently avowed. It was followed by secession as a logical consequence. It is very remarkable how rapid was the change in public sentiment. This new doctrine of the rightfulness of slavery swept over the whole Southern States in a few months, politicans philanthropists, ministers, suddenly starting up to find that they had been all along in error in thinking that slavery was an evil, and hoping that some day it would be removed, that they had been wrong in speaking of being "opposed to slavery in the abstract," it was abstractly not wrong, but right; they had been mistaken when regretting the circumstances which made emancipation ought not to be desire. This change of sentiment an doctrine was not gradual, but sudden; it went with telegraphic speed. The reason was that events were pressing upon the aristocracy of the South and threatening its destruction. Slavery had ceased to be a dominant power in the Federal legislation, and the social state which rested upon it was trembling to its foundation. There was but one thing to be done, and that was the setting up of a new government, the corner stone of which should be slavery. And this was not accidental or capricious, but simply a necessity The state of society which was sought to be maintained had its origin in slavery, and slavery could not but be put in the foremost place. Alexander Stephens understood both himself and the matter which he had in hand when he told the people, and the world that they had hitherto understand this thing. Before, they had sought to maintain their social state and only tolerate slavery, they had not seen that all depended on it; here was the true corner-stone which former builders had rejected, but which they were now making the head of the corner. The secession was a foregone conclusion long enough before it actually occurred: it was so understood throughout the South by thinking men, and the sudden spread of the new doctrine on slavery was the necessary preparation for it.

He, then who does not take slavery into the account in his thinking on this war, has not begun to get a glimpse of what it means; he who leaves it out in the settlement of it, will not advance a step. Its origin was in slavery, its issue is to be found only as it is connected with slavery. There may be, as there has been, through the tremendous power of a vast prejudice, a thousand endeavours to avoid the issue, but events will sooner or later compel every man, whether he will or not, to look it in the face. We say prejudice for in this thing, as in all history has been the case, a name has become a well nigh boundless power. The interest of slavery has for a long course of years, and by a persistent endeavor, created a term of terrible significance, and has wielded it with prodigious force,--we mean the word "Abolitionist." History has known before a term made a watch word and changing a dynasty, but never was a word brandished with such effect upon a nations well being as this. Time was when South as well as North, to be an" abolitionist," a member of the Abolition Society," was not only no strange thing, but a position held by the the foremost men, and without a thought that they were amendable to even the slightest censure of their associates. Jefferson and Pickney, as well as Jay and Adams, were abolitionists in name, as well as in fact. Delaware, and Maryland, and Virginia had their Abolition Societies, and the best and greatest men were members of them. But in the course of years Slavery changed all that. The oligarchy awakened to the danger which threatened it, and at first gradually, and them by more and more open effort, these societies were assailed or suppressed, till they with the death of the great men who founded them, passed out of existence, no one perhaps knowing precisely how. Then began the storm of abuse and anathematizing directed against all who dared to hold, or at least utter sentiments opposed to slavery. "Abolition" and "abolitionist" was echoed and howled till men became pale at the bare sound, and considered it the last and most dreaded terror to be called by the hated name.

But a change vastly more rapid in its movement is now taking place in an opposite direction, the significance of which we have but just begun to measure. The mind of the whole nation has been directed now for one year, with great steadiness to the contemplation of slavery from an entirely new stand-point, and divested of the cloud of prejudice which has for nearly a century, been thrown over it. The word abolitionist has lost its secret potency.

In this line of thought the present attitude of our government is of immeasurable importance. We are as likely to undervalue as to over estimate events which occur just beneath our eye. A few weeks since President Lincoln sent quietly into the houses of Congress a message of strangely straightforward character, clothed in very plain and homely garb, but of meaning not to be misunderstood, and admitting of no misconstruction. It asked that Congress should simply resolve that the government was willing to lend its aid to any State of the Union which should desire to bring slavery to an end. That was all. But that simple message marked an era in the history of the world, and will be looked upon in all future time as one of the grand events of this century. It was unlooked for, sudden, so that the country stood confounded for the moment, but the next was ready to adopt it. It quickly became the policy of the government and of the people, without, so far as we know, a single voice of moment raised against it. The people have not yet begun to understand all its great meaning. What is it? It is that the government of these United States deems slavery an evil, wishes it to cease , and will do what it can to help it to an end. It is the first time in all our history that this was true. The government has never so spoken before. Henceforth its policy is to help emancipation . It is a risen sun, it has brought a day whose glorious light we have not yet appreciated. Hereafter all its patronage, and power, and prestige will be thrown on the side of freedom, and no man can accurately measure the result.

The President has, by this great act of his, lifted the moral sense of the nation to a position to which years could not otherwise have brought it. It was one of those strokes of God-inspired genius which once in a century or so, changes the face of the world. Like many other acts of this truly great man, it was wonderfully timely, put forth at the moment, the fulness of time, it was not too soon, it was not too late. The sense and the thought of the people needed to be advanced up to its reception and had not wildly gone beyond the point of wisdom, the moment with a deep intuition was recognized, seized upon, and by a few words talismanic, the forming elements were crystallized. So they will remain. For all the coming time this people will look forward to the abolition of slavery. Freedom is the American watch-word, freedom for all men.

But a few weeks have gone, yet the change is wonderful already. The atmosphere is clearer and purer. The writer of this is living in a slave state, and is able to mark the changes better than those in places more remote from the influences of slavery. While a few months since no prominent men or class of men would venture to plant themselves openly on the platform of emancipation, now there is a great party forming in this state, (Delaware,) and at the coming elections in the autumn of this year, it will go into the canvass with Emancipation for its watch-word. The stigma which slavery has succeeded in attaching to the word "abolition" is already passing away, and it is no longer dangerous to one's reputation to be considered an emancipationist.

What is true in a slave state will be as true everywhere in the land. The presidential word has brushed away a world of sophisms, and settled a thousand pleas against dealing with slavery; it has declared not only expedient, but possible, immediate emancipation. The abolition of slavery in the District of Columbia following so quickly upon the message of the President, and the adoption by Congress of its recommendation, have made its words facts and demonstrations. Slavery has been abolished with a word, and in a moment, over a whole district of country --here is a fact to make the ages sing over in this land. We do not even think of the fifteen hundred or so captives set free; they are as nothing, except as occasions for the bringing into existence the momentous and glorious fact that this government is on the side of freedom, and its strength will be given to it henceforth. It is difficult to measure the import of all this, even as it is difficult to foresee the sweep of a mighty current which has just begun to rush in a new channel; that it is destined to sweep slavery from this country, no one now can have a doubt.

Hereafter the thinking on the subject of American Slavery will be only in one line--how shall it be done away? If we would have an understanding where a few weeks may advance us, we have only to remember what was the point of thought in relation to this matter. It was, how shall slavery be kept from extending itself. We were content to let it live if it did not subjugate other lands, but the events have crowded us far beyond that, we have gotten past a thought of it, no living man fears now, or even dreams of it, it has simply gone forever out of a sane man's mind. What an advance a year has made! We have been hurried past the place of argument against slavery. We are done with all that; the books and the pamphlets, the documents and the statistics are growing quickly obsolete, for they have done their work; we need not be careful of them for our future use. We shall not need them except as relics of a well fought field.

Those of us who have for a life time been doing what we could to hasten forward this day, who have spoken and written and suffered for it, in the new atmosphere which we breathe are like men that dream. We know that it would come, we hoped to live long enough to see the day. We see it and are glad, we did not think to see it soon, it has come so suddenly, it shines so broadly and with so rich a promise that we recognize it as God's day; we see his wonder-working power moving marvellously, making--was it ever shown so before?--the wrath of man to praise him; we behold how God has taken the work into his own hand; how he has made slavery destroy itself. More than human wisdom, and beyond human guidance is here, the thick night would not have gone so wondrously had not He rolled it away, we hail the light. This is the day the Lord hath made, we will rejoice and be glad in it.

But like all of God's gifts, it demands work and gives responsibility, responsibility and work proportionate to the boon.

He has given us a day, but it brings with it work of which perhaps we have gotten only a mere glimpse. It is well that we should endeavour to understand and appreciate what that work is, for it is no holiday that He has given us. We have asked in many a prayer that it might come, and having come we must see what is to be done, and manfully deal with it.

It is easy to talk of emancipation, but he has thought loosely and ill who sees no great difficulties in bringing it to a happy issue; who has not questions arise in his mind to give him pause when he contemplates a social change so vast in state of a race of twelve millions of men. Let not the reader suppose a mistake in the figures, we mean twelve millions, and not four; there are, indeed, four millions of slaves to be made free, but a change is to be wrought in the social state of the eight millions of the whites, which is only less than that of the blacks. To alter radically, to remodel the whole social fabric of a great and numerous people, to shift the foundation stones, remove them, and place others in their palaces, without racking the edifice or tumbling it in a hideous ruin, is the work of no inexperienced or careless architect.

The gigantic war which has been desolating one half of this land, has been, as we have said, simply the mighty frantic effort of a social state to establish itself; of a peculiar civilization to consolidate its power. The result of the war will be the total defeat of this attempt; the very endeavor, the waging of the war has shaken its foundation, its end will remove it entirely. This civilization, whose basis is slavery, has chosen to risk its existence on the issue of the war: it must accept the alternative which it has raised, and be content to pass away.

The war will decide the question of slavery, and with it alter the whole form of society at the South which rests upon it. But one civilization cannot pass away and leave a vacuum; one state of society cannot cease and have no other in its palace. It is only changes, not new creations which take place in the social world; one civilization gives place to another; society passes from one state into another . We are, then, on the eve of a mighty change, perhaps the greatest ever seen in the world before. That it can or could take place without an awful struggle, pangs which are the birth-thores of a nation, let no one imagine; that it will be done in a few brief months is impossible. While we write, victories have just been gained, the great city of the South has passed into the hands of our army, and men begin to predict the speedy downfall of the rebellion; but, alas, we cannot felicitate ourselves with any such prospect. The great class which has made the war to maintain its existence, will not consent to die thus; every element of human nature in its fallen form is against it. It will yield to nothing but simply irresistible force, it will die only as it is killed. We confess, as we look over the whole ground and weigh well as we can the origin and caused of this gigantic war, to a feeling, not of despondency or uncertainty, for we believe that God will one day bring it to a happy end, but of heart-sorrow and care, even as a woman has sorrow and foreboding at the inevitable agony ere a man is born into the world. To lift twelve millions of men to a new better place, to open before them a good and happy future, instead of certain prospective woe and final dissolution, is a work worth the tears and groans of a nation, and they can well afford to be patient till the time has come. At present let not one's heart fail him if the horizon grows dark and hope seems at times blotted out; let him remember well what the meaning of the strife is, that it is no accident, but the death-struggle of a civilization two hundred years old, and based on all the worst and strongest elements of human nature. It can have no easy death.

Taking it for granted, then, that a great change is about to take place in the social state of the South, and taking it for granted that slavery on which it is based must, under the pressure of the forces which are bearing upon it, pass sooner or later away, a point which we are not disposed just now to consider even debatable, a great question comes up, What shall be the future condition of the colored race in this land? How shall the problem be solved? What shall be done with the slave? Hasty and inconsiderate persons may find ready answers, but it seems to us that just now there is no question of so great intricacy, and certainly no one of equal moment to which an American can address himself. We propose in the remainder of this article to discuss it. It is not a subject on which it is well to dogmatize; we have learned that there is room for a very wide diversity of opinion; the most that any one can hope to do is by discussion to endeavor to elicit light. After all the

Providence of God will do the work; it is for us to be abreast of that Providence, ready to accept the trust and do the work which it assigns us.

We have dwelt thus long on the causes, and what we consider to be the true meaning of the war, because only by a right apprehension of them can we be prepared to deal with this great question. Those who are at the head of the government appreciate it most fully, and the President in his message frankly intimates that the only true hope of a lasting settlement of our national difficulties must be found in the ultimate emancipation of the blacks. But aware of the objections which must arise to the setting free of four millions of slaves and their remaining in the country, he proposes that a system of colonization shall be inaugurated by which they may be removed. Emancipation with colonization in lands provided for the freed slaves, is the scheme.

Without dealing with this proposition of the President in detail, let us look at the state of the case, and ask, Is colonization possible; and if possible; it is necessary, or even desirable? By colonization we mean, of course, the removal or deportation of the blocks to another country. We do not mean emigration; that is an entirely different thing.

We may ask at the outset, Have we a right to send out of the country the emancipated slaves? However it may have failed to be his country, this is his home, and by what law of morality shall you compel him to abandon not only his, but his father's and his ancestor's home? It is his by a line of descent stretching, in most cases, far back of theirs who talk so glibly of his colonization: and after, by a great act of justice, you have raised him from chattelhood into citizenship, and have given him a country, by what rule of right do you propose at the same time to banish him from it? A right-minded man will hesitate before he leaves the feelings of four millions of hearts out of his calculations. It is, we think, an element somewhat to be considered, and yet one utterly ignored by the most of those who talk on this subject. If it be answered, the colonization is to be voluntary, they only going who choose to go, we have only to say that that is not the true meaning of the terms, nor what is by common consent understood by it. If merely emigration is intended, and it is made no part of the scheme of emancipation, the case is altered radically. But of this more by and by.

Of the possibility of the deportation of the freedmen, a thoughtful man will have many doubts. The shipment of the natural increase for one year of our present slave population, sixty thousand, (60,000,) would tax the energies and resources of the nation to an extent which they who talk of it have not very fully measured. And then the original 4,000,000 remain. To those who have been accustomed to advocate the removal of the colored race from this country, we recommend a matter-of-fact calculation in ships and money and time. It will be both interesting and profitable; possibly it will impart some new ideas on the matter. For ourselves, we may say that we deem the proposition for the deportation of a race of four millions, with a yearly increase of sixty thousand, a wild dream, one of the emptiest that a sane man cares to entertain. The history of the race has never known such a thing; it has seen the emigration of millions, but the sending of them never.

But passing this, is the colonization of the colored race in this country desirable or necessary? For the entering upon a work so gigantic, even were it possible, there ought to be reasons the most imperative, absolute, and pressing. Mere opinions, theories, or prejudices, will not be sufficient; the demand for it must be made to appear with sunlight clearness.

What are these reasons? To us it does not seem easy to exhibit them. It is easy to declaim about the inferiority of the race, the impossibility of their ever living on an equality with the white race, their lack of ability to support themselves, and the like, but in the end it is very difficult to perceive the logicals consecutiveness of the argument. The inferiority of a race can hardly be shown to be a valid reason for its banishment from the presence of the superior, and by its power; the inability of a people to care for or to elevate themselves, does not seem a precisely good argument for sending them to a new land, and to a naked dependence on their own resources; the invincible prejudice of the white does not at once give a very potent, at least a very just reason why the black should be expatriated.

We will not assert it, but there is good cause to suspect that while in the minds of perhaps the majority of those who for a few years past have been active supporters of the colonization scheme, the good of the black and of Africa have been prominent motives, yet it had its birth and its chief support in the way in which it bore upon the interests of slavery. The presence of free blacks among slaves is an element of weakness in the system, and though it may not have been openly avowed, yet there is too much reason to suspect that colonization was intended vastly more for them than for freed slaves. It was a scheme to strengthen slavery, and it ceased to elicit sympathy or generous support so soon as it appeared to give no promise of that result.

Asking the reasons for colonization, we apprehend that when the argument is pressed, it will be found to terminate, if on any thing substantial, upon the benefit which it will confer on the black race. Without volunteering the details of that argument, which, indeed, we do not profess to see clearly, we may say that there is at least a preliminary question, whether or not that end cannot be better attained without colonization than with it? Is it not possible better to elevate and to do good to the colored race in this than in any other land to which they may be sent?

But we are writing coolly, as if this were an open question whether the four millions of blacks are to remain for many years to come in this country or not. It is no open question. They are here, and here they must remain for a period which no man is competent to limit, even in his argument. They cannot, or to speak mildly, they will not be transported across the sea or to any foreign land. They may eventually, as we shall endeavor to suggest, go, but they cannot be sent away. In this assertion, we leave the inclinations and the will of the black man out of the question. There are reasons which must operate on the side of the white to make it impossible. The colored race is necessary, and will be so for a period indefinitely long, to the southern country. It constitutes its labor; it is the productive force of that land; it has been for the past two hundred years. It is the foundation element of the whole social state. Now by what power shall there be a speedy removal of the whole labor of a country? How shall the entire producing element be suddenly abstracted? Were that possible to be done, the whole state would plunge at once into poverty and ruin. Once or twice the experiment has been tried, in historic times, of banishing or destroying a producing element of a state, and though done on a comparatively small scale, the result are sufficiently marked to teach all after time. Spain did it when she drove the Moors from her Castilian lands. France did it when she murdered and banished the Huguenots, and they both have scarcely, after two and three centuries, recovered from the shock and the ruin.

But we need not spend our space in discussing the point. However any one may deem the colonization of the whole colored race desirable, still it will remain an impossibility; there are natural and economic forces which would be omnipotent to prevent it. They are needed here, and where a race is needed, there, in this age of the world, it will abide. There is work to be done; they can do it, they have done it; there is no one else at present to take their place, and so a power above wishes, prejudice, or argument, holds them here--the power of an economic necessity.

The colored race is here, here for a long time it will remain; it will not--the events bewildering us by their rapid march all point one way--it will not remain in slavery; it will and must by-and-by be free. We, as an American people, must accept this double truth with all its difficulties and perplexities; we must like men, in God's fear and with many a cry for his help, bravely deal with it. We need not now go back and stand sighing over the past, and mourning that we did not a century ago meet it and escape the mighty work and sorrow of to-day; we cannot put it away any longer; the great questions rise up before us with a menace upon their brow; they demand and they will have an answer now to-day. No scheme of deportation or colonization shall open any easy door of escape; let no man console himself that the question of emancipation is to be solved by any such short and simple process; here on this continent, within the borders of these States, slavery has done its work, and just here freedom is to have her greatest and most glorious triumph. This American State has given some examples to history, it has given some demonstrations of the power of free institutions for the white, it is giving to-day its most memorable, and is it too much to hope that it will yet give to the world a more glorious, because more difficult, demonstration of the same power in the black race? What if it should remain, for it, after having completed its work for the one, it should crown it in the other, by lifting it from deepest slavery, and by self-sacrifice and toil make it a blessing to the world! So we believe it will yet be. The way is not clear now; the people do not see their work; but by-and-by it will of itself be before them, and they will address themselves to it, bringing every quickened power which marks them among the nations, and, under God, they will complete it.

How it shall be done we do not feel competent to intimate, and it was not the purpose of this paper to attempt to indicate. No man, perhaps, is sufficient for that. The Providence of God we believe will mark the path, and events will hurry us if we be ready to follow them in right line of the work.

There are some things, however, which may be said that may possibly cast some light upon the supposed difficulties of the matter of emancipation without colonization. These difficulties, we think, arise in many cases from a mistaken estimate of the negro character and capabilities.

It is not our design to enter upon the question of the inferiority of the race or the impossibility of its ever living on an equality with the white; while we are not ready to grant the first, certainly not to the extent to which it is pushed, we are disposed to believe the latter. It is doubtful, we are inclined to believe it impossible, that the two races can ever on this continent abide on terms of social equality. We are, too, inclined to believe that this country is not to be the ultimate home of the colored race. It will go out from it. We think that there is that in the character of the African race which makes this probable, perhaps certain. In the strange workings of Divine Providence this race has in a marvellous manner been brought to this land, and put under a tutelage for a great future, and that Africa, its home, may become the recipient of blessing, the foundation and preparation for which were made in this country.

The bondage of the Israelites in Egypt was not an accident, but a divinely ordered procedure, which had a striking bearing upon the character of the Jew and shaped his whole after history. It was a work of preparation, and it was not done in a short time, but took two or three centuries to be brought to perfection. American slavery, like this Egyptian bondage, will have its results on the future or Africa.

In saying this, of course no reader will suppose that there is in the thought a justification of slavery, any more than when speaking of the great benefits which flowed from the bondage in Egypt to the Jew, we justify the selling of Joseph, or the tyranny of Pharaoh. It is God's wonderful work to bring the greatest good out of the deepest evils; the Fall to issue in Redemption.

It is impossible to discuss the future of the black people in this country without immediately being brought into contact with the future of Africa. The one is closely connected with the other. The movements of Providence are synchronous. How wonderfully events are prepared in distant places, that they may be brought together at the appointed moment! The fact that at just the time when the great and absorbing questions which relate to this people in our own land are forcing themselves upon our attention, the continent of Africa is attracting more of interest in the way of discovery and travel than any other portion of the earth, has, we think, a meaning.

Geographical research has almost exhausted other lands, while here almost a continent, at least till within a few years, has remained unexplored. This has not been because no efforts have been made to break through the thick veil that has always hung over it. Travellers have been unceasing in their attempts to penetrate into the interior, and have failed, not from want of energy, but because of the insuperable difficulties in the way. If they have succeeded in reaching the shores, they died under the fatal coast fever. If they have escaped this death, and pressed towards the interior, it has been only to fall victims to savage beasts or more savage men. So that African exploration has been, until perhaps within the last fifteen years, a history of melancholy disaster and sacrifice of valuable life.

Of late, new and marked success has crowned the efforts made to lay open this continent to the knowledge of the world.

What has been accomplished will strike with surprise any one whose attention has not before been called to the facts of the case. Let the reader take a well prepared map of to-day and compare it with that from which he studied his lessons a score of years ago. He will remember how simple and easy to be remembered was the information to be conveyed by that wide and lightly-colored track which bore the words, "Unexplored Regions ." It embraced the largest portion of the whole continent. But this has been encroached upon year after year, on the South by Livingstone and Cumming, on the North by Barth, on the East by Barton, and on the West by Wilson and Du Chaillu, until the discoveries have almost touched each other. Wide stretches of thousands of miles, given up hitherto in the thoughts of men to perpetual desolation and drought, have been shown to hold vast inland seas, deep navigable rivers, and to be teeming with animal life, populous with men and faithful of all the products of tropical luxuriance. So Africa begins to be known; by-and-by it will be opened up, made ready, we think, to link its history with a people on the other side of the ocean.

Leaving the point as proved, that the blacks are to remain, at least for an indefinite period in this country, (we do not say that it will be forever, but of this we shall speak in another place,) we naturally ask whether there is anything in the African character that is possible of future progress and elevation. We answer unhesitatingly, there are natural characteristics which will in a very marked and peculiar way be a means of their speedier rise.

It has been the misfortune, if so we may call it, of the African continent and the African people, to present their worst and most repulsive aspects first. This is the case with the country. The coast to which the voyager comes, for the most part lies low, and everywhere in its teeming bottoms disease and death are lurking. If he escapes the one he never avoids the other. The "African Fever" on the West coast is the certain welcome of the new comer, the only question is whether he will survive it. The incidental mention which the missionary traveller, Livingstone, makes of his thirty-seventh attack of fever, and Du Chaillu of his fiftieth, and the exhaustion of the last of fourteen ounces of quinine which he had taken on his journey, are ominous of the inhospitable reception which the country gives. But as soon as the traveller passes inland he comes into an entirely different region. Towering mountains, snow-capped and forest-crowned rise before him, and down through their passes healthful and bracing winds are winds are blowing, wide champaigns already full of uncultivated fruitfulness, or grass and bush-covered tracts, which nature seems to exult in filling with animal life, in its most beautiful, as well as gigantic and ferocious forms, everywhere appear. While at first it would seem as if here were a continent capable of doing little or nothing for the world, fit only to give, as in the past, a little indigo, ivory and palm oil, borne on the backs of degraded natives to the coast, we find that it is in reality a continent already producing unassisted harvests of cotton and sugar, and some of the products most necessary to man, and only needing that development which Christian civilization can give, but has never given, to bring it into the closest sympathy, and for good, with the rest of the world.

What is true of the Africa continent has been emphatically true of the people. The world has always seen the African race in its lowest form. This seems true as far back as Egyptian monumental times. One is struck, when looking at copies of ancient hicroglyhics, with the degraded type of negro feature which always appears when these captive people are delineated. The African race seems to have been fated to be always represented by a slave, and, as was inevitable, it has been judged by the example seen. But the researches of travellers have, of late, compelled us to reverse many, if not all these conceptions. Africa, gives us indeed, perhaps the lowest types of humanity in the Bushman * or Hottentot, yet the explorations of travellers have also shown these are not true and normal examples of the African stock.

*Even these Bushmen seem to have suffered in reputation from their observers. "Those who inhabit," says Livingstone, "the hot sandy plains of the desert possess generally thin, wiry forms, capable of great exertion, and severe privation. Many are of low stature, but not dwarfish; the specimens brought to Europe have been selected, like coster-mongers' dogs, on account of their extreme ugliness; consequently English ideas of the whole tribe are formed in the same way, as if the ugliest specimens of the English were exhibited in Africa as characteristic of the entire British nation."

It can readily be seen that whatever the African character is measured by the standard of an African slave, the judgement must necessarily be an erroneous one. The best tribes are not, in the nature of things, those out of which slaves are made. The bolder, more energetic and intelligent are those who make slaves. War and conquest are the fruitful sources of slavery; they have been in all age, in every country, and are so today in Africa. But the abler tribes are the warriors and the conquerors, while the weaker and the lower are the captives. Thus at the outset the slave declares by the fact of his servitude his inferiority of lineage.

To this we are also to add the pretty well-known fact that the poorest of these captives are those who came into the hands of the slave-dealer on the coast, while the better made and the more intelligent are reserved for the service of their captors. Thus, with this further reduction, you have in the African as he comes to the slave-ship, the lowest specimen of an inferior type of his people. But just these have been the exponents of the African race, and it is not only not surprising, but entirely natural that a false estimate should have been made of the whole negro family.

What we would infer, the exploration of recent travellers show to be actually the case. Within the limits of a single article such as this, it is of course impossible to traverse the whole ground. We might, however, refer to the Caffrees in the south, close upon the regions where the Hottentot is found, a race of stalwart and noble men, who have had skill and bravery enough to resist the power of the Dutch, and even to wage a determined war with the English power itself. To the east of these, Dr. Lindley, one of the missionaries of the American Board of Commissioners for Foreign Missions, found tribes among whom he lived for a quarter of century, and whom he describes as being physically inferior to no race, the men in some districts averaging nearly six feet in height. "They might be called stupid," says Livingstone, (p.21,) speaking of Bakwains, a people with whom he was much associated in South Africa, in "matters which had not come within the sphere of their own observation, but in other things they showed more intelligence than is to be met with in our own uneducated peasantry." Two of the missionaries of the American Board, Messrs. Preston and Adams, speaking (Missionary Herald , 1856,) of a visit to the Pangwees, a very extensive tribe of people living just under the Equator and back from the coast, and who are described by other writers as an every way superior race, tell us of natives whom they saw from places still farther inland "which we had heard of, but as yet had been unable to reach." "The variety," say they, "of complexion presented to us was quite an object of curiosity. Some were of a jet black, others with their braids of soft black hair, one and a half, or two feet in length , might be easily mistaken for quadroons." The New American Encyclopedia treating of the Mandingoes, a West African race, says: "They are remarkable for their industry and energy. They are mostly Mohammedans. The principal trade of that part of West Africa which lies between the equator and the great desert is in their hands. They are not only active and shrewd merchants, but industrious agriculturists, and breeders of good stock of cattle, sheep and goats. They are black in color, tall, well-shaped, with regular features and wooly hair. In character they are amiable, hospitable, imaginative, credulous, truthful, fond of music, dancing and poetry. They are adventurous travellers, extending their commercial journeys over a greater part of Africa. The Mandingoes are the most numerous race of West Africa, and have spread themselves to a great distance from their original seat, being found all over the valleys of the Gambia, Senegal and Niger." Such quotations and testimonies might be multiplied, were it necessary, but enough have been exhibited to demonstrate the fact that there are superior races of men in Africa, that these are even the characteristic races of the continent. Every new discovery exhibits this more clearly. The negro as he has been seen in the slave transported to other countries is no true type of the African man, but the continent is peopled by races capable of high attainments and indefinite civilization.

Though the negro of this country may not be of the best races of Africa, yet he is not of the worst, and as we shall have occasion to remark, he has had influences exerted, both as to race and character which much more than compensate for any possible inferiority of descent. We may fairly take the estimate of the native African as we find him at his best estate at home, and build a promise of the future of the African here upon it.

The African character has its own marked and distinctive peculiarities. It is tropical. It has passion deep and pervasive, slumbering within a rounded form and in deep dreamy eyes. It is ductile and plastic, ready to receive impressions and to be shapen by them. It does not posses the hard, aggressive features of the character of the tribes of Northern Europe; it does not seek by conquest to extend its power, or to mould other people to its form.

It is adapted to receive rather than to give. It is therefore essentially imitative. From this comes the rapidity with which under favorable influences, the African advances in civilization. Wherever these influences are numerous and powerful enough to be the most prominent, the negro yields to them with marvellous rapidity.

There is, perhaps, no race that gives up so readily and fully old habits and associations. We find no granite formations of character underlying the race, such as are met with in the tribes and peoples of Asia. Compare, for instance, the plastic mobility of the Pangwee and Bakwain with the rigidity of the Hindu or Chinese. Or where the case may be seen in even a more striking way, compare the African negro with the American Indian; take the one from his tropical wilds, the other from his forest home, and place them both under the same civilizing influences, and where at the end of a fixed period will you find them? In a single generation the one is nearly at your side, the other is simply a savage still.

The rapid rise of the negro race in the West India Islands, Jamaica, for example, when made free by the British Government, is a very striking illustration, though the time has been too short to bring it out to the full. Taking all the facts as they are given us, we find the people rising almost at once, (for thirty years are usually as nothing in the life of a people,) out of the barbarism of slavery, into a nation self-supporting, self-governing to a considerable extent, moral and religious, not, indeed, in the highest degree, but still wonderfully advanced. * We believe that it is without a parallel.

*See Sewell's "West Indies, or the Ordeal of Free Labor in the British West India Islands," an evidently dispassionate and disinterested view of the condition of these islands. An attentive consideration of his stateements would go far to relieve the matter of emancipation of some of the difficulties with which to many it seems environed. "These people," he remarks, "who live comfortably and independently, own houses and stock, pay taxes and poll votes, and pay their money to build churches, are the same people whom we have heard represented as idle, worthless, fellows, obstinately opposed to work, and ready to live on an orange or banana, rather than earn their daily bread."

Together with this plastic docility, the African has another which at first sight seems in flagrant contradiction;--the race has a peculiar power of resistance permanence. It is said, probably truthfully, that no race has ever been able to abide a close contact with the Anglo-Saxon. One of two results has always followed;--either it has been swallowed up and lost as a river in an ocean, or it has gone down and been swept away. But this race has neither been absorbed nor destroyed. It has grown under the most adverse influences, and asserts itself in all its peculiar characteristics under foreign skies, and after the lapse of two centuries. The negro of America is a true African still.

This race has not greatly mingled with other races. It is, we are inclined to believe, rather a characteristic of it not to seek an amalgamation with another people, its tendency is to remain apart. We are well aware, indeed, that this is exactly contrary to the views of many who have built their opinions on popular assertions and prejudice rather than on observed facts. The assumption is that the negro desires to mingle his blood with that of the white races. The reverse is the fact. There is, though it may seem to some unaccountable, a certain pride of race, which leads the negro to exult in the purity of his blood, and to regard a foreign element in it as not only not desirable, but even objectionable. This feeling does not belong simply to the negro on his own continent; it perpetuates, perhaps magnifies itself when surrounded by another people. Among them in this country a pure-blooded negro will, with biting sarcasm, taunt the mulatto with the fact that the blood of another race is in his veins.

This feeling, which must have been noticed by any one whose observation has been extensive or intelligent enough to collect the facts, leads the race to remain by itself; and when left to its natural course, such is the result. The statistics of this country show that the free black does not and cannot mingle with the white race. No elevation or freedom can produce such an intermixture. Here and there, but so seldom as to present but perhaps a single case only in widely separated communities, there is an inter-marriage. This seeming want of inclination, coupled with a natural and insuperable repugnance on the part of the white, must ever keep the two races apart when they stand on an equal footing of freedom.

The often repeated argument against emancipation, founded on the notion that it would be necessarily followed by amalgamation, is the product of the grossest ignorance and thoughtlessness, while at the same time it betrays a shameful want of confidence in the white race itself. It surely argues no great power or stability in a people when they are not able to keep themselves from being mixed up with a confessedly inferior race. But facts point in a wholly different direction: so far from freedom promoting this intermixture, the only condition in which these two races are found mingling is where the negro is in a state of servitude. Here the process goes on freely and under the working of natural causes. The influences which on either side under other circumstances make it impossible, here become inoperative, and are overborne by other and more powerful ones. The close intimacies, beginning with infancy and extending over the whole life, destroying what under other circumstances might seem to be a natural separation; a servile desire to please on the part of the slave, lust and cupidity on the part of the master, all combine to make the blood of the two races flow in the same veins. Slavery is the source of amalgamation. The mulatto and the quadroon tell you unerringly of a present or a former servitude.

With this pliant ductility and this permanence of race, there is another striking characteristic;--the negro's attachment to place. It is probably a natural trait, but from easily perceived causes it is perhaps intensified in the case of the American negro. He loves his home and seldom goes willingly away from it, whether slave or free. The number of fugitives from bondage would be prodigiously multiplied were this feeling more easily overcome. Many a poor bondman has turned back to slavery when the hard alternative has been forced upon him to remain in it or go forever away from the familiar and dear scenes of his childhood's home. It is necessity scarcely less powerful than death that compels him to leave them behind.

The efforts which philanthropy has made to promote their colonization have met with an insuperable obstacle here, and will be compelled to contend, more or less unsuccessfully with it, till there shall be strength and education enough given the black to rise above it.

Among the many objections which have been urged against emancipation, this has been a very common one, and has had great force in the popular mind;--it will flood the Northern States with free blacks. The objection is vulgar and thoughtless. If the simple economic law of supply and demand, as powerful over men as materials, were not sufficient to keep this people where they are needed, and to prevent them from going where they are not, the love of home would be strong enough to bar such result. The slave needs all the mighty stimulus of a prospective deliverance from slavery to induce him to leave the place of his birth, and that even is often enough; why, then, when he has that boon in his hand, and walks the old haunts a freeman, with work requited and enough, why should he now go away to strangers and strange land? No, the States which have meanly and and disgracefully passed their laws excluding the freed black from a home within their borders, might have spared themselves the dishonor. The dreaded calamity would never have occurred. The enactments were the assumption of a gratuitous infamy.

The effect of emancipation will be the reverse of this fear. Instead of the freed slaves flocking northward, the free blacks of the North will gradually go South; in place of Northern States being overrun with the one, they will, in process of time, be stripped of the other. With slavery out of the way, the black will naturally bend his steps to the region where climate, congenial employments, habits, associations, all welcome him; he will go away from a people who do not understand him, and whose prejudices keep him down, to be near a people who have grown up with him, who know him, and are better able to do him good. This consolidation of the race in one part of the land will have an important bearing on its future. Emancipation only will fully accomplish it.

Passing these characteristics, common to the race both in Africa and in this country, let us consider others, which have been superadded by the residence of the negro in America. These are marked and important. The residence of the Jewish people for some two hundred years in Egypt, had a controlling influence over the whole national character and destiny. The Hebrew would never have been the man he was, nor would he have had the after history had he not known the bondage in the land of the Pharaohs. So, we think, the negro will, in all the coming time, be a man essentially different because of these two hundred years of slavery in America. * Nor will it be a temporary or limited effect; it will probably mould all the history of the race on its native continent. Africa will in future times look back upon slavery in America much in the same way that the Jew did upon his Egyptian bondage, and will be able to trace the wonder-working power of Divine Providence in the results which have flowed from it.

*There are some curious analogies between the bondage in Egypt and slavery in America. It seems as if slavery were about to come to an end in this country after almost identically the same period of existence. As far as the best calculations can fix the time, the bondage in Egypt lasted something more than two hundred years, and it is about that time since the first cargo of African slaves were landed by the Dutch at Jamestown, in 1620. The Hebrews went out suddenly and unexpectedly, under the pressure of tremendous judgments Will it be so in America?

Strangely enough, one of the marked effects of the residence of the black in this country has been to give a new and foreign element to the mental and physical structure of the negro. It has created an admixture of blood with a superior race. The natural effect of slavery has been to infuse the best blood of the master in the veins of the slave. This fact has not, perhaps, received the attention which it deserves as having an influence upon the future of the negro race. We do not speak of it in the way of sarcasm or reproach, but as something which, while it cannot be concealed or denied, ought not to be overlooked. It cannot be when the coming history of this people is under consideration.

The intermingling of race has been extensive; so much so, that in many places the pure-blooded negro is in the minority of the whole colored population. Here is not the place to make any extended observations on the intellectual and physiological effects of the union of different races in the same people, to elevate and give them tone and character. The facts are very familiar. We can see that in the case before us these effects will be of the same general character.

In the new social order which will come into being on the abolition of slavery, this intermixture of race will be less and less frequent, but what has already taken place will tend greatly to hasten the elevation and advancement of the black. The energy, the fire, and activity, the ingenuity and perseverance of the Anglo-Saxon, joined to the plastic docility of the African, is a strange combination, yet one which may be seen every day, and which when made free and permitted to exert its unrestrained power, will be of unmeasured value. The mulatto makes a very bad slave, Anglo-Saxon blood being never intended to run in the veins of a voluntary bondman, but will be a noble freedman.

It need not be a perpetuated intermingling of race. It will not be when slavery has gone, and it is well. Physically the mulattoes are a feeble people, and destined usually to an early death; nor are they prolific. By the force of merely natural causes, in process of time, they will almost wholly disappear. The immobility of the race will assert itself. But in the meanwhile they will have done their work in assisting the rise of their brethren. It is a force imparted for a special occasion. strangely given, but not in vain. It is a spoil taken from the enemy, one of the marvellous instances in which human passions and crime go to help human progress; it is the blood of the master given to make by-and-by a speedier elevation and a more perfect manhood for the slave.

Together with this transfusion of lineage in a part of the colored population, the actual contact of the whole with the white race is another fact which must be attentively regarded. This otherwise isolated people, isolated not only by continental separation, but by color from the rest of the human family, have been brought into the closest possible relationship with one of t he foremost people of the world. They have been introduced into families, making part of the household; have, to a certain extent, been brought under the influences of the civilization and enlightenment of this white race. Upon such a susceptible people, receiving impressions so easily, and being moulded so completely by them, this association cannot but have an unmeasured influence, hastening their elevation whenever the time of freedom comes.

In a state of slavery, while these influences are exerted and their power is given, yet it must be more or less a latent power. Slavery gives no opportunity for its exhibition. It is like throwing electric sparks into the Leyden jar; it might seem that as they flash and disappear, that all the power is lost, but when the proper conditions are fulfilled the unseen force, slowly gathered, puts itself forth with prodigious energy. When the impulse and opportunity is given by freedom to the American negro for advancement, the probabilities are that an example of rapid elevation will be given by them such as the world has never seen. The elements which have been working in and around them are such as have never been combined in any people before. The facts are, when thoughtfully considered, not only peculiar but wonderful. Here is an imitative and plastic people dwelling in the most intimate associations with an enlightened, energetic race, surrounded by the light of civilization, learning, art, science; it is simply impossible that they shall not partake in some degree of these great benefits. They may be seemingly excluded from them all, but a subtile power is the while going forth and is silently laying itself up in store, by-and-by to appear in their sudden development.

But beyond and above all, the negro race in America is a Christian race. Here are four millions of Christians. We mean, of course, Christian in contradistinction from any other form of religious belief. Before this one fact we may stand in silent wonder and admiration at the processes of God's great providence. If any where on earth the night of heathenism is dark, and the darkness is palpable, it is in the negro's native home. Yet here are millions of the same race maintaining their peculiar characteristics with great distinctness, yet in all essential points a Christian people, infinitely above their brethren in their original seat. The contrast in this regard between the race here and there is simply immeasurable. They have been taken out of the blackness of idolatry, and nurtured for two centuries in the light of an advance Christianity, so that heathenism has passed almost out of their traditions.

All this great result has been occasioned by slavery, sprung from cupidity and the origin of unnumbered crimes! Perhaps human history presents nowhere a more striking example of God's power to make the wickedness of man bring honor to his name.

Here, then, are a Christian people, with very much of superstition, with very much of ignorance, with, you may say, a low type of piety, but yet, after all, a Christian people. They are more, a Protestant people. Romanism has never obtained any extensive hold on them here. * May we not say that in this, that these four millions of blacks are a Protestant Christian people, there is an element of unbounded promise?

*It is very striking in this connection that Romanism has never made any progress or met with any permanent success in Africa. In the North where Mohammedanism prevails, (see Barth,) it is repudiated on account of its supposed proclivity to polytheism, and in other parts of the continent different causes have prevented its taking root. Indeed, West Africa presents the most striking instance on record of the utter failure of the Romish religion to benefit a heathen people. For more than two centuries the Portuguese had a kingdom in Congo, and for a time it was powerful and extensive in its influence. With it the Papacy sought an establishment. "It was a work," says Wilson, (Bibliotheca Sacra, Jan . 1852), "at which successive missionaries labored with untiring assiduity for two centuries. Among these were some of the most learned and able men that Rome ever sent forth to the Pagan world. It was a cause that ever lay near the heart of the kings of Portugal, when that nation was at its climax of power and wealth. Yet before the close of the eighteenth century, indeed, for any thing we know to the contrary, before the middle of it, not only all their former civilization, but almost every trace of Christianity had disappeared from the land, and the whole country had fallen back into the deepest ignorance and heathenism, and into greater weakness and poverty than had ever been experienced even before its discovery." With a continent wonderfully kept from Romanism there, and a people preserved from it here, may we not see a divine adaptation for the future, a finger-pointing to some signal good for the church and the world?

If we throw together these characteristics and facts in regard to the negro race which we have now pointed out, we have this:--Here is a nation with good mental endowments, peculiarly distinct and seemingly destined to remain so, yet docile and ready to receive the impression of all influences surrounding them, brought not only in closest contact with one of the first races of the world, but actually receiving a transfusion of its best blood, made at least in part partakers of a very high civilization, and already Christianized in a form where there is the least play of superstition or error. Is it difficult to predict the future of such a people? Is it certainly absurd to say that there is a history before it, if not of the highest style, yet one good and even excellent; if not the noblest, as aggressive in its good upon the world, yet one sufficiently glorious for itself?

Whatever may be the ultimate destiny of this people, we think that we are justified when we say, looking over the facts in the case, that when they have removed from them the incubus of slavery, and start forth on a career of freedom, that their rise will be extremely rapid. Indeed, taking all the elements of progress which they possess into consideration, it is simply impossible that it should be otherwise.

While we give expression to these thoughts, let us not be

understood as affirming that the benefits of which we speak are the legitimate results of slavery. Nothing could be farther from our intention. To substitute a cause for an occasion is a very common error: indeed some minds seem incapable of fully apprehending the world-wide difference. The legitimate effect of slavery is to thrust the victim as far down in the scale of being as is possible. The nearer the brute, the better the slave , is the true law of slavery. Slavery is the cause of ignorance, degradation, and crime. It, by a dreadful necessity, strips the slave of every attribute of manhood; neither soul nor body is his own; the one is kept in darkness as the other is sold in the shambles. What can a system that locks up all human knowledge, stalks through the soul trampling down all that constitutes the man, not accidentally, but by the necessity of its existence, what can such a system do for its victim?

There may be benefits such as we are now speaking of, coming to the slave in his slavery, but slavery does not give them. The laws which create slavery would shut out every thing, but they cannot. In spite of them all, the good will come. So it has been with the colored race in this country. This good can only be made to appear in a state of freedom.

Just here there is forced upon us another thoughht of tremendous significance. This gradual unseen, but mighty gathering of power in the slave in this land cannot be forever without one day coming into form. You cannot be evermore throwing electricity into the jar; by-and-by its overcharged contents will burst out in sudden explosion. While you may let the conductor take them safely and usefully away! No one cares to follow in imagination where the thought leads him. Emancipation must be given sooner or later, or all goes down in a hideous ruin; and no experience can calculate nicely when the last moment of safety is reached. It may come, and the crashing thunderbolt tell that it has gone.

Of the way in which this freedom is to be brought about, it is not the intention of this article to speak. To this writer, there seem perhaps no problem which approaches it in difficulty. Emancipation--it is easy to talk and declaim about, it is easy to prove right and to show desirable, but how to bring about, that is the labor. He is a rash man, who speaks very confidently on this matter. That it should be brought about, that the well-being of the two races, the interest of two continents, and humanity itself, the very existence of this American people demand it, no thinking man ought to doubt. It becomes this nation to address itself to this work, and see that it is done and done well.

While, however, we stand aghast at the difficulties of the work, it is comforting to know that the solution is not committed to us, but that the providence of God is pushing it forward. Events crowding upon each other with a rapidity which bewilders us, seem steadily and swiftly bringing the freedom of the negro to its accomplishments. No man is competent to say what the issue will be, or to what new form the events will shape themselves. A little while ago the most common consent of men looked toward a gradual emancipation, to-day it seems more and more as if the fetters were to be stricken off at a blow. How, or when, who shall say?

In whatever way it is done, one thing we may expect--it will not be by the premeditated devices of men. The great works of God are not done in that way. Smaller and comparatively unimportant ones may be, but those which affect grand interests, and shape the history of the world, the Great Jehovah takes into His own hand and brings them to pass so marvellously that all men shall recognize His power and "Know His name," (Isa. 52, 6.) "Therefore they shall know in that day that I am He that doth speak; behold it is I!" In the meanwhile it becomes all men reverently and obediently to be watching the movements of His Providence, to keep abreast of them, and boldly to take each new step as it is indicated, and as soon as it is. The end may come sooner, as it probably be vastly easier in its coming than we have dared to hope.

Taking the fact of emancipation as fixed, and to be realized, and that there will here be a race of freedom rapidly rising civilization and enlightenment, we are confronted with the question-- Is this country to be the ultimate home of this people ? We answer, No. We do not believe that this people were brought here that they might have a permanent residence. They were brought to this land for tutelage and trial. The Hebrew bondage is the example illustrating it. Whatever may be said in respect to the right of the negro to a perpetual home here, and we would be the last to dispute it; whatever may be urged against the prejudice which thrusts them out of association and into painful separation, and we would not for an instant justify it; yet still we are of the opinion that here the negro will not abide as a people. Social equality and the enjoyment of every right are well nigh hopeless for him. Were there nothing else in the way, the stigma of slavery is almost perpetual and ineradicable.

He is here, not for America, but for Africa. He is here for a training that could not have been gotten there. When it is complete, he will go back and make the continent what it could never do without him. When, under the influences which have shaped his character and built him up, he has become a self-reliant, advanced Christian man, and he is ready and able to do something for his race, he will go back to do it.

Then will be Africa's time. Exploration, advancing commerce, and with it Christianity, will have prepared the way, as we see it now being made ready, and the negro race of this land will go back gradually but with increasing rapidity, and by a natural and healthy emigration. Such emigration only could be permanently and extensively beneficial to a new land. The colonist must be more or less be impelled by the native force of his own character to seek the new home. Africa must look for her Christianity and her civilization especially to her own sons. Like all other lands which are to be elevated, the power raising her must come from without. It seems to be the course of Divine Providence that new and heathen countries are to be civilized and Christianized by Christian colonization; not commercial, but Christian colonies must go out to them. The colonists must not supplant and destroy the aboriginal inhabitants, nor must they come simply as teachers, but they must abide as those whose home is to be there, who as residents bring them the arts and practices of civilized and Christian life, and whose extended and continued example illustrates the power and benefits of the life they bring.

This has been for the most part of the course of events. No people rises alone and unaided from a state of barbarism. The early history of nations which have a history, usually begins with the coming of a colony, whether it be Phoenician, Cadmean, or Trojan. "Religion, law and letters are not indigenous, but exotic; in all the past career of man upon the globe one race hands the torch of science to another." Of no people must this be more true than of the African. If Africa is to be elevated, it must be by the infusion of life and power from without, and by means of colonies which bring with them the elements of life and power.

The colonist who brings this boon to Africa must be an African. Every year and every experiment renders this more clearly evident. The white missionary has done, and is doing, a noble, perhaps indispensable work, but the permanent results which are to be found over extensive regions must come from men whose race is similar to the people among whom they dwell, and with whom it can mingle freely and advantageously. Such a race has been preparing, and will be prepared by the overruling power of God in this country.

At present the work of preparation is not complete. A few have been made partially ready, some fit for the work have gone and, by their success on the west coast of Africa, have shown what the people are capable of doing. A beginning has been made, but in the coming time it must have a new starting-point. The Liberian colony, or any other which shall be formed, must rise from the position of a far distant place to which one is banished, to be the attractive spot which calls, and to which a manly energy and independence urges.

To send only the degraded and the low in intellect is not the method to elevate and ennoble a new land. The stream will not rise higher than the fountain, and a slave, though free, cannot at once be a truly self-reliant man, least of all can he be a good teacher of self-reliance and progress. He must first teach himself, well as he may, before he can do much for others. The colonist must, if he carry good with him, be first elevated himself. Nor, on the other hand, can the isolated and exceptional cases of advancement and cultivation be spared from their brethren here.

For the most part, as can easily be seen would naturally be the case, the colonists who have hitherto gone have been the most energetic and intelligent. But in the time to come such cannot all be spared: their example and aid are needed here to help the general rise. But if the time comes, and when it comes, that under the stimulus of freedom the colored race as a whole advances to the point which we think there is for it in the future, individuals will not be of account; emigration passing along the track of commerce, and commerce by its own great laws will set toward Africa, and in this way the problem of Africarn colonization, and of African history in America will be fulfilled. All this may be very distant, many years may go by, though, fewer than perhaps we may imagine, but the Great God who guides the hours and their burden can bring it all about, and through one of the deepest crimes of history, the Rebellion of to-day, hasten it in its coming. It will be like Him to make crime its own avenger, and both crime and vengeance illustrate his goodness and love.

###

www.ingramcontent.com/pod-product-compliance
Lightning Source LLC
Chambersburg PA
CBHW062028280526
45787CB00005B/2252